Looking for Love, I found Joy

Rachita Nikam

BookLeaf Publishing

Presentation by *BookLeaf Publishing*

Web: www.bookleafpub.com

E-mail: info@bookleafpub.com

ISBN: 9789358310313

First edition 2023

I dedicate this book to all those who have lost their way amidst the chaos that surrounds us. I dedicate this book to those who help us on our way back. This book is for the healers, the children, the dreamers and the explorers.

Follow the light and come back home.

ACKNOWLEDGEMENT

This book was inspired by all the authors I have read growing up, my teachers, my friends and my family. They have all had an impact on my mind and my soul. Without them, this book would not be possible.

I would also mention Ludo, my 3-year-old puppy, who lies on my lap as I work on this publication. He saved me!

I want to specifically take the time to mention my father, Nitin Nikam. He introduced me to the world of words at a very young age. He inspires me to go on and stand up every time I fall down! This book would not have been possible without you, Dad!

PREFACE

Be happy with what you have
Make peace with your lot
Eat whatever is served in your plate
In the end,
It is all Destiny and Fate

Action Potential

Come and Go
with the light, you meet the dark

Ebb and Flow
start a fire, without a spark

High and Low
no difference ever so stark

You reap just as you sow...
Every action will leave its Mark!

Habits/Addictions

Each and every one
Every person on this planet
We all struggle with addiction
It's just that for each
it's a different drug, a different vice

Some are addicted to buying stuff
for others it's gambling
Some are compulsive liars
and a few guise it as religious rambling

People have the usual addictions
some are tolerated more than others
Caffeine, Nicotine, Weed
a little hit here, a little puff there
that's all they need

Some addictions don't appear
to be addictions at all
Needing to be right
attention, affection, love, sex
Some also just love to fight

So what makes a habit an addiction?
I guess for that people turn to their *moral voice*

But as you ponder that question,
let me ask you this,
What is <u>your</u> drug of choice?

Hoodwinked

And I did not
Could not
Swim back to the Light
Swim back to the Shallows

After I had explored
the Deep
Waters of my Consciousness

But maybe,
I did not want to
Because you see
there cannot be...

A wave,
without a pull!

But how could you
know, you could not
see my eyes
from under the wool!

Bubbles

Floating bubbles, through the air
catching light, technicolored rainbows
Glittering with the breeze

Bubbles,
have always been a joy
always bright, light as air
filling us with ease

Freedom though,
these bubbles represent
try, as some might
one can't hold on to these
bubbles, they don't stand still
nor freeze

You may try to fit yourself in one
make it so that
that's all there is
in your sight
the bubble will bust eventually
leading you to your own release!

The Joy of these bubbles lies with the observer
The bubble itself has no might

it's their POP that makes us giggle
the dissolution of these bubbles
our minds appease

Lingering Thoughts

Words fall apart
Sensations linger ...

My roots, mistaken as shackles
turned them into chains
How silly of you!
My roots, nourish me
especially when it rains

My worth isn't yours
to determine, to assess,
contemplate and decide

Time is the only,
I repeat, ONLY, judge
It turns like the tide

Before you disrespect, disavow and disintegrate
Before you point a finger
Look within yourself, explore inwards
Words they fall apart, but sensations they linger

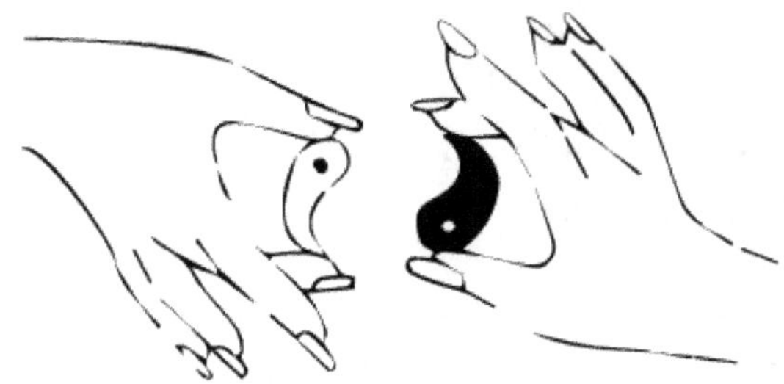

Locked in my head

I have a room inside my head
Sometimes I wish you could see
If only there was a lock
So I could give you the key

You could see
How bright and blue
the sky is to me

I would show you my thoughts, my dreams
like stallions, running wild and free

Just don't go towards the the corners
No matter what,
or how strong the urge may be

Those hold my darkness
the shadows and the haze
the daze you perceive
the craze, I carry within me

On second thoughts,
I have a room inside my head
that I am glad no one can see
I'll keep it locked,
it's only for me

Juxtaposition

Words are a tool
words are a weapon
poetry the language of the fool
But if you were wise
Would you learn the lesson?

Everything and everyone is in perpetual
conversation
In those quiet moments, we find eternal
salvation

Shadows aren't the dark
They only appear with light
Differences that are stark
But do you see
All that is in your sight?

Everything and everyone, in perpetual
conversation
Those quiet moments, a reprieve from the
damnation

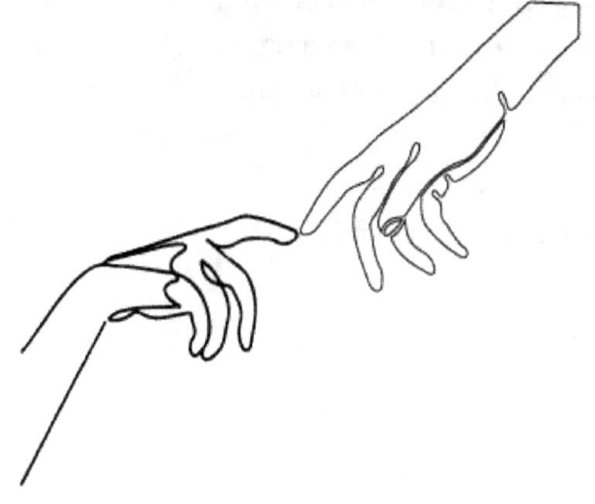

Absence feels eternal

Sometimes absence
can stick to your fingers like gum
more suffocating than a presence
trying to breathe, in vacuum

You can avoid this
ignore it make yourself numb
pack it in boxes
tape it up, lock it in the back room

Facing it headfirst, however,
is easier said than done
the intricacies of your spirit, your soul
the entangled web of feelings entombed

You will rise on the other side
For every day comes with the sun
Letting someone's presence into your life
is opening your heart to pain, forever doomed

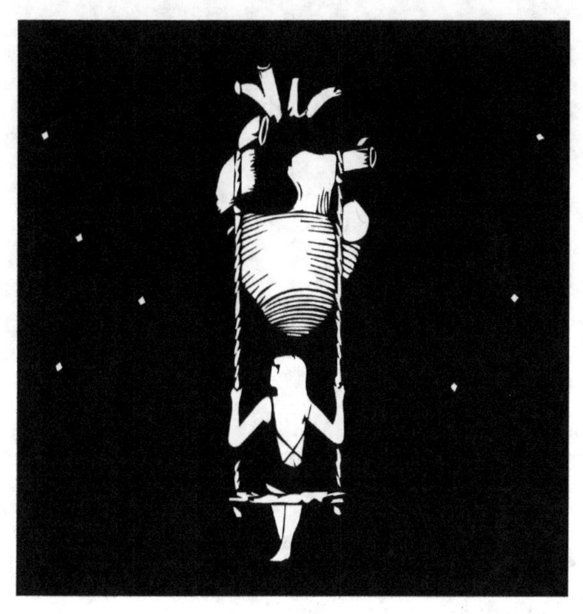

Tightrope

Walking on a tightrope
Hope held tightly in one hand
Faith, landing loosely in the other
Grief I carry in my heart
Freezing me in place
Taking just one step, not another

The soul searches for a home, to rest
but what's this heavy immobile weight on my
chest?
My bucket of grief is a never-ending well
For multiple lifetimes, in it, I could dwell.

but Life, it's like walking on a tightrope.
Hope in one hand, and Faith in the other
Do Not let grief smother
that Inner Light, never, nope!

Burn brighter every time you hear the call of the
abyss
Love harder, call the people you miss
because Life is like walking on a tightrope,
Hope in one hand, Faith in the other
grief may be an endless well
but *Joy* will take you farther!

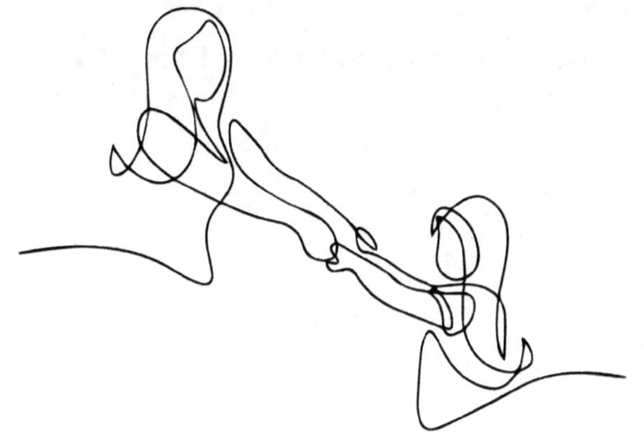

An ode to Love

I love you

Are these the three most powerful words that
exist?
Love follows you through life
And the people you leave behind carry this love
in your absence

But love... It's a tricky thing.
Like water, it'll take the form of the container it's
served in

So when mom says she loves you, It's a very
different thing
Than when a friend says they love you
Which is different,
From the sweet nothings a lover whispers into
your ears

With great power comes great responsibility
Said Uncle Ben

Love can inspire
It can also destroy
Being open to love is

Equivalent to being open to pain
And to hurt
But not in vain

In all its vulnerability love can be beautiful
In all its vanity love can be toxic

It's simpler things that fill my heart with
sunshine
If the world was a better place
If I were a different person
These words would be inconsequential
But it isn't

And so
The most powerful words for me become

'I see you'

Rooted Wings

I have wings on my heels
And roots in my heart
If I had to choose between the two
I would not know where to start

My wings take me to the clouds,
The sky, the moon, the shooting stars...
Taking flight when my mind wanders;
Oftentimes just because...

My roots offer me a home,
A place to rest, a place to heal.
Accepting my weird, twisted lores,
no need to hide or to conceal...

Roots ask me to stay
To while the day away...
Wings, though, they choose to soar
Even when the skies look gray...

Together, they exist
within my soul
Making me complete
Not half, but a whole

I have wings on my heels
and roots in my heart

But if I had to choose between the two
I would not want to start

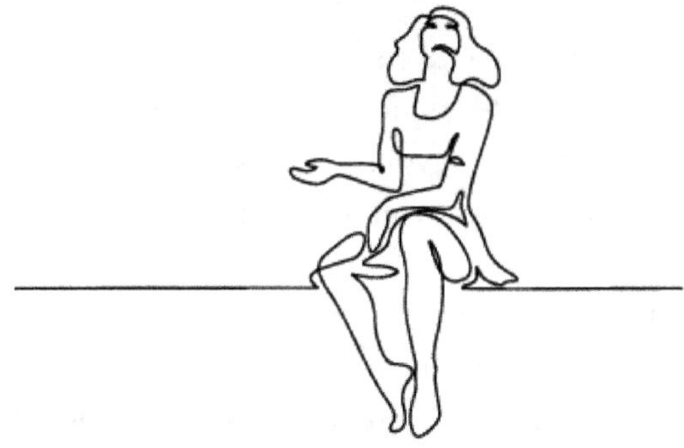

Elemental Interactions

I believe each human
Is an element of their own
And when they meet, a reaction takes place
You can feel it in your bone

When hydrogen meets with chlorine
You have the formation of a strong acid
Don't let that fool you, simple as it looks,
These reactions are anything but placid

Some reactions are more complex
Than what meets the eye
Caustic soda and hydrochloric acid give us salt
and water
An essential reaction, one cannot deny

Some reactions need external energy to work
Some reactions exude energy- that's a good
perk!

No this isn't a chemistry lesson, The point here
is
it isn't the elements that cause the reaction
They each need what they need,
Cannot stay in limbo, forever in inaction

Each human is an element of their own
None are good, None are bad
It's how they react to one another
And that should be known

Definition

The world will incessantly ask
For you to define yourself
Who are you?
They'll ask; what makes you happy?
They'll wonder...

Are you a cat or a dog person?
Mountains or beaches?
Sunrises or Sunsets?

But would you ask the wind
What color is it?
Would you try to define the shape of water?
Would you ask the Eagle,
Why does it love to fly?
Or the Myna, what makes her cry?

You become Every thing you touch
Every one you meet
Every place you go
But, nothing can change much
the soul within
the Home you know

You are everything and nothing

all in one breath
A soul trapped in time
The universe in its depth

Spiral Fractals

And if everyone was just
looking out for the SELF
no one would be putting
an elf on the shelf

To build something that stands the test of time
we need people
we need love
we need art
Needing isn't the crime

Is life really as linear as we believe it to be
If you thought of it as a circle
wouldn't you be free?

Dream in a Dream

Many moons ago
I stumbled upon a dream
It was shiny
It sparkled with Joy
It ripped my insides at the seams

So precious
So wanted
I decided to keep it safe
Locked in a box
Tucked in a corner
Without a way to escape

The dust settled, and the years passed
It was decades later, when I was asked

"What makes your heart beat faster?
What makes you feel alive?
Is there something that makes you glow?
Something that puts your heart in overdrive?"

'YES!' my soul screamed
from the deep recesses of mindless despair
'Yes, there's that one dream...
 save it, fan it, it's running out of air'
So one bright summer morning, I gathered all
my courage
Ventured into my mind
Picked up the box, wiped off the cobwebs
Terrified of what I'd find

My dream leapt out!
Shining, sparkling, glorious still
Adding joy, laughter and wonder
my own fount of magic
to take my cup and have my fill!

Inner world

I carry within me
A world
Of people and places alike

My world includes
Blue skies
Pink clouds
White rivers
And black sands

It includes
Peace, love, and rock & roll
And holding hands
People laughing

My world includes
The sun, the moon, the stars
The entire universe
And your smile.

I carry within me
A world!
of people and places alike
Of people and places I like

Being

Yes....
Inherently
Irrevocably
Undoubtedly
Ecstatically
I want to be...

Stupidly
Clumsily
Unequivocally
Unabashedly
Wonderfully
I am!

Possibilities

For the first time in my life,
I don't have a plan
I don't know where I am headed
It isn't ideal, but I'm not sure I'm not a fan

For the first time in my life
I don't have a goal
There's no restlessness inside of me
No anxious burning in my soul

For the first time in my life

I don't have a plan
I don't have a goal
To tell you the truth, it makes me feel more
human
It makes me feel whole

For the first time in Life
I don't have a path to follow
The first time I don't have a plan
The whole world lies waiting for me
I can do Anything I want
and Everything that I can

Time and again

34

Everything in time...
but,
What is time?

Some call it a band-aid, Others a cure
Would we meet?
If I told you where,
without the when...
Isn't time just a cruel joke then?

I think, Time is mercy
Time is flavor
to be savored

Tell me, are you
someone who passed through time?
or does time
pass through you?

Schrodinger Friends

You exist
so clearly in my mind

Your music
Your words
Your faces

Yet when one seeks
They cannot find

Those moments
That love
Those places

Like Schrodinger's cat,
Existing in a box...
Locked away!
Safe?

Always there, never around
Not lost, but never found

Finally Found

At the crack of Dawn

Light meets Dark
Grief meets Love
Anxiety meets Intuition
Fear meets Compassion
Intention meets Action
Breath meets Life

And
I meet You

www.ingramcontent.com/pod-product-compliance
Lightning Source LLC
LaVergne TN
LVHW010827200726
843508LV00012B/2523